DATE DUE

Catch Me If You Can!

-Text and photographs by Densey Clyne-

Gareth Stevens Publishing

MILWAUKEE

Insects — a vital part of life

Insects are important to life on Earth. They are the main food source for countless **species**. They **pollinate** plants throughout the world. They recycle decaying plants and animals.

This young frilled lizard survives by feeding on insects, such as flies.

Words that appear in the glossary are printed in **boldface** type the first time they occur in the text.

This desert beetle usually **forages** for food at night. But here it is crossing a sand dune in the daytime. It might be eaten by a lizard. Imagine how enormous other animals would seem if you were shrunk to this beetle's size.

Insects are small and plentiful. Many bigger animals **prey** on them. Lizards, frogs, birds, and some small mammals eat insects. Yet insects are the most successful creatures on Earth.

How have insects managed to survive in nearly every **habitat** and *evolve* with so many shapes and life-styles? Part of the answer is in this picture. Look carefully at the fallen leaves. One of them is not a leaf, but an insect. Here's a clue: it has two pairs of wings.

Over millions of years, insects have developed strategies to keep from being eaten by their enemies. One tactic is to not look like a typical insect. A bird searching for a juicy mouthful is not interested in eating something with a face like this.

Now you see me, now you don't

Another tactic insects use to guard themselves from enemies is **camouflage**.

Thanks to camouflage, a hungry bird might not see the insect — a young flower mantis — on this ginger plant (*above*). The shape, color, and petal-like legs of the mantis resemble parts of the flowers.

Many insects become almost invisible by seeming to melt into the background. Stick insects look like sticks and stems. The spiny leaf insect (*above*) looks like leaves.

Spiny leaf insects feed on several different plants, including blackberries and roses, but they are hard to see in the **foliage**. They are usually a solid green or light brown, but some, like this one, wear **mottled** camouflage colors.

This leaf looks as though it has been nibbled on by a caterpillar. Actually, it *is* a caterpillar eating a meal.

This caterpillar belongs to the family of moths known as *Geometridae*, which means "earth-measurers." Its more common name is *looper*, or inchworm, because of the way it loops along as if measuring with each step.

When it is not looping, it has some special disappearing tricks, such as the one in the picture *(above)*.

How many caterpillars are in the picture (above)? Three? No, four! The three little furry ones are using a big smooth one as a bridge. The smaller caterpillars do not need to hide from **predators**. They are covered with irritating hairs that make them an unpleasant mouthful. Birds soon learn to leave them alone.

The big caterpillar has to keep still and rigid, looking like a stem, if it wants to stay hidden — even if the tiny feet of the other caterpillars tickle as they go across.

Every time this caterpillar **molts**, it saves its head capsule. It then stacks the empty capsule with the others on its head. The idea is to make the caterpillar larger and unrecognizable.

Wings: not just for flight

Insects are the only **invertebrates** that have wings. With wings, insects can find food, catch prey, communicate danger, frighten enemies, seek **mates**, and move out of harm's way.

A dragonfly, like the one *(above)*, can fly very fast — up to 50 feet (15 meters) a second — so it can escape from most birds. Simply by taking off from its resting place, a winged insect can get away from non-flying enemies.

The leaf-eating katydid (*above*) does all its feeding, moving, and mating in the safety of darkness. By day, it rests and tries to be invisible to its enemies.

The katydid's wings are the same shape and color as a leaf, and its long legs are the same color as the stems.

But it is not enough for an insect to look like its background. It has to behave like the background, too. A katydid positions itself like a leaf on a plant and stays very still. Even the slightest movement could catch the eye of a bird.

Can you see two moths in the *top* picture? They blend in with the lichen and moss on the tree bark. These moths belong to the *Geometridae* family, like the caterpillar on page 8. During the day, they keep very still, pressing their outspread wings against the surface of a tree trunk. At night *(bottom)*, they are active.

In the desert, there is not much vegetation to blend in with, so there are few insect hiding places. That is not a problem for this small grasshopper. Its speckled pattern matches the sand (*above, left*). To disappear completely, it shuffles part way under the sand (*top*). Only its eyes and **antennae** poke out, alert to danger.

Making eyes at the enemy

Look at the face on page 5. Here it is again
(*above*), but it is not a face at all. What you are
looking at is a pair of eyespots — not real eyes
— on a hawkmoth caterpillar.

When a bird or lizard sees these eyespots, it
thinks they belong to a large animal, so it does
not attack. This caterpillar's real face is
actually tiny, hidden away under the segment
at the front.

An emperor moth can rest safely in daytime because it has large, false eyes on its wings. If a bird comes near, the moth spreads its wings, revealing the "eyes" to frighten the bird away.

Many types of moths, caterpillars, and a few other insects use this "false-eye" strategy to trick predators. But if too many animals had false eyes, predators would probably no longer be fooled by the trick.

Insect cover-ups

Some insects protect themselves with armor plating. A beetle's front wings, for example, are not used for flying. Instead, they act as protective covering for the insect's soft body and delicate wings.

Few birds would tackle this scarab beetle (*above*) with its tough armor and six spiky legs. Ancient Egyptians regarded one type of scarab beetle as sacred and a symbol of **immortality**.

The casemoth caterpillar weaves a cover, or case, from silk thread and bits of twigs. This case is thick and tough but allows the caterpillar movement, too.

The case has a hole at each end — one at the top for taking in food and one at the bottom for getting rid of waste. The silk thread comes out of a pore below the caterpillar's mouth.

Weapons of attack and defense

This bulldog ant (*above*) moves around freely, night or day. Its weapon is a pair of jagged **mandibles** (mouthparts), with which it grabs small insects. It then stings the insects to death for food.

Even a fierce predator like this has a few enemies, however, such as larger insects and lizards. Sometimes the bulldog ant must use its mandibles in **self-defense**.

A tropical weaver ant, or green ant, grips its victim with sharp mandibles. It then injects an irritant fluid from the tip of its abdomen into the victim. You can see the fluid in the photograph (*above*).

To a human, this feels no worse than a sharp pinprick. To an insect, however, this could mean death — especially if other ants arrive for a mass attack.

Wasps are often red, orange, or yellow combined with black. These colors are a warning sign to predators that the wasp's sting can injure or kill any animal that tries to attack it. This "fair warning" tactic is common among insects. It helps protect both prey and predators.

Unlike the wasp, a honeybee cannot use its stinger to protect itself. That is because when it stings, it dies. The stinger gets pulled out of the bee's body, killing the bee.

In the photograph (*above*), a spider has caught a honeybee in its web. But the bee has stung the spider to death. The bee, too, has died, either from the spider's bite or from stinging the spider.

Wearing false colors

As we have seen, some insects protect themselves by looking like a part of their environment. Some harmless insects trick their enemies by looking like a dangerous or awful-tasting species.

The gentle longicorn beetle (*above*) has orange-and-black stripes. This makes it look more like a wasp than a beetle.

In addition, its rigid front pair of wings are very small, like a wasp's. The delicate hind wings are held high, like a wasp's. To its enemies, this harmless beetle is considered to *be* a wasp.

These newly hatched insects (*above*) are the young of a green katydid, but they look more like ants. Most predators avoid eating ants, so looking like an ant has good survival value. This is especially true for plant-eating insects that must move often and quickly to find enough food. Some young stick insects and even some adult insects also **mimic** ants.

The insect (*above*) looks like a honeybee, but it is not. It is actually a harmless drone fly, sometimes called a bee-fly.

These flies visit flowers to feed on nectar, which is exactly where honeybees are most often found.

The drone fly behaves like a bee. It also looks like a bee. This tricks predators that might otherwise enjoy a tasty fly into leaving the bee-like creature alone.

Chemical weapons

Many insects use chemical substances to protect themselves. For example, gumtree sawfly **larvae** (*above*) produce a blob of sticky fluid in their mouth. The powerfully scented fluid smells like eucalyptus and keeps predators from approaching.

If attacked, a tiger moth *(left)* produces repellent fluid in front of each wing and displays its bright red body color.

The cupmoth caterpillar *(right)* defends itself with stinging spines. Each spine acts like a needle to inject an irritant chemical into predators.

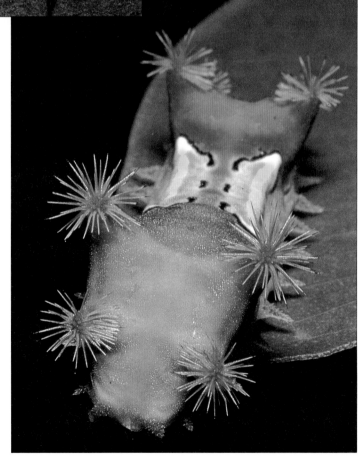

Butterflies usually fly slowly and are quite visible, so they are easily caught by birds. The monarch butterfly (*above*), however, can glide and soar without a care in the world. Only an inexperienced young bird will attack it.

The secret weapon of the monarch butterfly is in the poisonous sap of the milkweed plants on which its caterpillars feed. The sap does not harm the caterpillars or the butterflies. It builds up in the butterflies' bodies and can make a bird that eats them very sick.

A fiddle beetle picks up pollen from a flower.

Insects are a vital part of life on Earth. They supply food to many types of animals and plants and are an important part of the food chain that sustains all life, including humans. If insects became extinct, all life on Earth could vanish.

A tree cricket feeds on a mantis egg case.

29

Glossary

antennae: a pair of thin, movable organs on the head of insects and other animals that are used for touching and smelling.

camouflage: a way of disguising something or someone to make it look like its surroundings.

evolve: to advance through stages of development slowly and gradually.

foliage: the leaves on trees and other plants.

forage: to search for food.

habitat: the place in nature where an animal or plant lives and thrives.

immortality: having an unending existence.

invertebrate: an animal, such as an insect, that does not have a backbone.

larvae (plural of larva): the wingless forms of newly hatched insects.

mandibles: mouthparts on some insects that are used for gripping and biting.

mate (n): the male or female of a pair of animals.

mimic: to imitate or copy.

molt: to shed an outer covering.

mottled: having patches of different colors or spots.

pollinate: to place pollen (tiny spores) on a plant.

predator: an animal that hunts other animals for food.

prey: an animal that is hunted by other animals for food.

self-defense: the act of defending oneself.

species: a group of beings with similar characteristics that are of the same type and that mate together.

Books to Read

Animal Survival (series). Michel Barré (Gareth Stevens)

Ingenious Insects. Anthony Wootton (Biblio)

Insects Do the Strangest Things. Leonora and Arthur Hornblow (Random House)

Look Again! A. J. Wood (Dial)

Nature's Tricksters. Mary Batten (Sierra Club)

The New Creepy Crawly Collection (series). (Gareth Stevens)

Wonderful World of Animals (series). Beatrice MacLeod (Gareth Stevens)

Young Naturalist Field Guides (series). (Gareth Stevens)

Videos

Adaptation of Survival: Insects. (International Film Bureau)

Animal Camouflage. (Phoenix/BFA)

How Animals Survive. (AIMS)

Planet of Life: The Insect World. (Discovery Channel)

Tell Me Why: Insects. (Prism)

Web Sites

info.ex.ac.uk/~gjlramel/classtax.html

info.exeter.ac.uk/~gjlramel/anatomy.html

aruba.nysaes.cornell.edu/ent/biocontrol/info/primer.html

www.bos.nl/homes/bijlmakers/ento/begin.html

Index

For a free color catalog describing Gareth Stevens Publishing's list of high-quality books and multimedia programs, call 1-800-542-2595 (USA) or 1-800-461-9120 (Canada). Gareth Stevens Publishing's Fax: (414) 225-0377. See our catalog, too, on the World Wide Web: http://gsinc.com

The publisher would like to extend special thanks to Jan W. Rafert, Curator of Primates and Small Mammals, Milwaukee County Zoo, Milwaukee, Wisconsin, for his kind and professional help with the information in this book.

Library of Congress Cataloging-in-Publication Data

Clyne, Densey.
    Catch me if you can! / by Densey Clyne.
    p. cm. — (Nature close-ups)
    "First published in 1992 by Allen & Unwin Pty Ltd . . . Australia" — T.p. verso.
    Includes bibliographical references and index.
    Summary: Highlights insects, the most successful creatures on earth, and their amazing tactics for survival.
    ISBN 0-8368-2056-8 (lib. bdg.)
    1. Insects—Behavior—Juvenile literature. 2. Animal defenses—Juvenile literature. [1. Insects. 2. Animal defenses.] I. Title. II. Series: Clyne, Densey. Nature close-ups.
QL496.C58 1998
595.7147—dc21   97-41450

First published in North America in 1998 by
Gareth Stevens Publishing
1555 North RiverCenter Drive
Suite 201
Milwaukee, WI 53212 USA

First published in 1992 by Allen & Unwin Pty Ltd, 9 Atchison Street, St. Leonards, NSW 2065, Australia. Text and photographs © 1992 by Densey Clyne. Additional end matter © 1998 by Gareth Stevens, Inc.

Printed in the United States of America

1 2 3 4 5 6 7 8 9 02 01 00 99 98